God in the Raging Waters

Other books in the Lutheran Voices series

See www.lutheranvoices.com

LUTHERAN VOICES

God in the Raging Waters
Stories of Love and Service
Following Hurricanes Katrina and Rita

Bishop Paul Blom

Augsburg Fortress

Minneapolis

GOD IN THE RAGING WATERS
Stories of Love and Service Following Hurricanes Katrina and Rita

Large-quantity purchases or custom editions of these books are available at a discount from the publisher. For more information, contact the sales department at Augsburg Fortress, Publishers, 1-800-328-4648, or write to: Sales Director, Augsburg Fortress, Publishers, P.O. Box 1209, Minneapolis, MN 55440-1209.

Editors: Kathy Haueisen and Susan Johnson

Cover Design: Koechel Peterson and Associates, Inc., Minneapolis, MN
www.koechelpeterson.com
Cover photo: Victims of Hurricane Katrina in boat near New Orleans. © Jim Bartlett/ Weatherstock®.com

ISBN-13: 978-0-8066-5317-4
ISBN-10: 0-8066-5317-5

Manufactured in the U.S.A.

10   09   08   07   06   1   2   3   4   5   6   7   8   9   10

Dedicated to the people of God in the ELCA
who have demonstrated what their baptismal calling
is about in their support and response.

Contents

Preface

Living along the Gulf Coast of the United States demands paying attention to weather forecasts on a daily basis, especially during the hurricane season. The season was particularly active in 2005. The National Weather Service named enough storms to use the entire list in the alphabet and then began using the Greek alphabet to name the last few storms.

When Hurricane Katrina made its way across parts of Florida and then reformed in the western Gulf, we took special note. When it became evident that it likely was headed for the Louisiana coastline and that the city of New Orleans was directly in its path, we began holding our breaths, waiting to see the outcome. I recall going to bed the night Katrina began to pound the coastline and awaking the next morning relieved to hear that the storm had moved out of the area and it appeared that New Orleans's levees had held. But within hours came the news that this was not the case.

The story of the horrors that followed captured the attention and the hearts of people around the globe, inspiring an outpouring of compassion as overwhelming in scale as the floodwaters themselves. The response came swiftly and forcefully to the offices of the Texas–Louisiana Gulf Coast Synod, as well. Our phones—all five lines—rang constantly with offers from near and far to help in any way possible. When we needed help just keeping up with the offers to help, I invited a retired pastor in the synod to act as an ad hoc coordinator of office relief efforts, and he agreed. Two weeks later, he came in to say that he couldn't keep up and needed more help. The Rev. Rob Moore, assistant to the bishop, stepped forward to take over the coordination role. He established an orderly process for tracking and responding to contacts and communicated information about what was going on in the synod via our website. Then he set up a separate Web site under www.futurewithhope.org. This is based on Jeremiah 31:17.

Today, we are blessed with leadership from the Rev. Kathy Haueisen, who assumed the task of coordinating ongoing recovery on behalf of the synod office as well as providing invaluable assistance with the book you now hold. The Rev. Tom Minor joined the staff of Lutheran Disaster Response/ Lutheran Social Services of the South (LSSS), and helps with coordination of "on the ground" disaster recovery along the Gulf Coast. Bernard Scrogin, Lutheran Disaster Response (LDR) staff, and a Lutheran Social Services of the South (LSSS) leader for a number of years, came out of retirement to help coordinate recovery efforts in Texas and Louisiana following Hurricane Rita.

By late spring 2006, financial support of more than $1.3 million dollars had been channeled through the synod. Some of the money has provided financial support for clergy and other church leaders whose congregations were, at some point, unable to pay salaries in the wake of the catastrophe. A portion of the money is designated to provide grants to congregations, enabling them to hire staff to assist with particular areas of ministry. Hosanna Lutheran Church, serving Covington and Mandeville, Louisiana, used a grant to add a children's ministry leader. These communities, where wind damage was severe but flooding was minimal, have seen a burgeoning population of families with young children. Similarly, in Baton Rouge, where the population doubled in a week due to the influx of evacuees, two congregations used grant money to hire a person to help coordinate efforts to reach out to new residents.

Money has been directed toward paying insurance deductibles for congregations that sustained damage of varying degrees, allowing them to move forward in the recovery and rebuilding process. Dollars also have been provided to help individuals and families meet immediate needs for car repairs and basic necessities as they struggle to get back on their feet after losing everything they owned. Additional assistance to individuals has been provided through the many, many gift cards sent to the synod from ELCA members throughout the country.

An extremely difficult situation following Katrina was further complicated when Hurricane Rita came calling less than a month later. While initial forecasts predicted that Rita would hit the coast farther south in Texas, the storm took a sharp turn to the east, placing Houston directly in its path. My wife and I joined those evacuating Houston, traveling to Austin to stay with our daughter and her family. Inching our way westward in bumper-to-bumper traffic, the trip, which normally takes just under three hours, took twelve.

Rita's impact along the Louisiana–Texas border added another level to relief and recovery efforts. LSSS, an LDR affiliate, is providing and coordinating resources, trained personnel, and experience to help restore bruised and broken lives. It was been a challenging task and will continue to be so for some time to come.

—Bishop Paul Blom, Texas–Louisiana Gulf Coast Synod
   June 2006

Introduction

"We do not know what to do, but our eyes are on you."
—2 Chronicles 20:12b

Disasters have happened for as long as there has been recorded history, and probably for centuries before we learned how to record history. When disaster strikes in any form—flood, famine, draught, fire, war, plague—God comes calling. God comes in the form of those who respond to a divine nudge to do something in response to the disaster.

We may not know what to do, but we know we have to do something. We come hardwired to respond to the suffering of another.

The first response is rescue. People show up with whatever is most needed—boats and helicopters, food, firefighting equipment, first aid, medical supplies and equipment. Others who cannot come in person send checks to organizations that respond on their behalf. The focus is on rescue. Get the people off the rooftops, out of the flood waters, into someplace safe.

The next step is relief. Relief workers meet the basic needs for food, water, shelter, clothing, and some way of communicating with others. People need help finding their loved ones. Again God comes calling in the form of people trained to respond to these emergency situations. Those on the front line are supported by others who may lack formal training but who bring compassion and a willingness to respond in many and various creative ways.

The final step is recovery. In our fast-paced culture, we underestimate considerably how long recovery takes. It can take many years. And we don't really ever get "back to normal." Rather, we adjust gradually to a new kind of normal. Every detail of life changes. It helps to have people walk side by side as advocates with us as we recover from our wounds. Each person's grief is unique, but the experience of grieving is universal. We need each other in the process. We take turns in the role of the grieving and the role of advocate for the bereaved. Since we are the body of Christ, when one member suffers, we are all wounded. And when one member heals, we all benefit.

Grief intrudes, frightening us and threatening our lives. Yet this unwelcome intruder also smuggles in an invitation to a new way of life. Our normal responses are revulsion, rejection, and protest over the loss of the life we had. Even if that life wasn't good, it was familiar. Yet, loss, of every degree and kind, contains a seed of possibility that invites us to reorder priorities, to express compassion more fully and openly, to redefine community. Pain often is a catalyst for growth and a greater good.

The biblical witness is full of this ebb and flow of loss and possibility. The climax of the story is, of course, the crucifixion, death, and resurrection of Christ. Talk about surprise endings!

The triple tragedies—Hurricane Katrina, the flooding of New Orleans, and Hurricane Rita—resulted in devastation unparalleled in this country in recent history. The recovery from this triple whammy remains a national event a year later.

For weeks we were riveted to the media images. We wept at the sight of people stranded on rooftops or walking through chest high polluted waters in search of safety or crammed like cattle into makeshift shelters. We were stunned by the magnitude of the tragedy and overwhelmed by the weight of need.

Yet, when the going got desperate, the faithful got going. This is the story of God in the raging waters. It is the story of how thousands of members—cells—of the body of Christ responded and how the body of Christ is still responding as, day by day, small step by small step, the journey to resurrection continues.

Where was God? We're not far enough from this triple tragedy to know what new life will be born out of this chapter of history. But we do know this—God was there in the raging waters. God was there in the boats and helicopters rescuing people off rooftops. God was there in the medical teams that set up impromptu MASH units at shelters. God was on the buses evacuating desperate people into "foreign lands." God was there in the millions of dollars donated to relief agencies. God was there in the thousands of volunteers who came bearing gifts of supplies, labor, and most important of all—hope.

And we know this: God is here now in hands and feet of volunteers who continue to provide hope, healing, and hospitality during the tedious work of putting in place a process for long-term recovery. God is here in the prayers of millions of people in the global village. God is here in the resiliency of people who live with the aftermath of tragedy, hour by hour, rebuilding their own lives while they reach out to help their communities build a new tomorrow.

God heard the cries and responded. This is the story of Lutheran voices on a journey with God, from storm and flood to rescue, relief, recovery, and resurrection. There is no "The End" to this story. The story of loss and grief is everyone's story, not just those touched directly by the storms. The story of new life and hope for the future belongs to all people of God.

1

The Beginning:
Storms and Sudden Changes

"Give ear to my prayer, O God; do not hide yourself from my supplication. Attend to me, and answer me; I am troubled in my complaint. I am distraught. . . . My heart is in anguish within me, the terrors of death have fallen upon me. Fear and trembling come upon me, and horror overwhelms me."
—Psalm 55:1-2, 4-5

On August 29, 2005, Hurricane Katrina tore through the Gulf Coast, leaving a swath of destruction from Texas to Florida, and wrecking havoc on cities that got in her way. While the rest of the nation watched in horror and helplessness, four of the levees protecting New Orleans from Lake Pontchartrain broke, flooding much of the city. Less than a month later, on September 24, 2005, Hurricane Rita ripped up the Sabine River that defines the border between Texas and Louisiana. Though millions of people in metropolitan Houston were spared, the damage from Rita was devastating to the "Golden Triangle," an economically depressed area that straddles east Texas and West Louisiana between Beaumont, Port Arthur, and Lake Charles. Like Katrina, Rita left people stranded in triple-digit heat without power, potable water, or a way out of the area when roads were rendered impassable from fallen trees and debris. High winds tore roofs from buildings throughout the region, allowing additional damage from heavy rains. Statistics published in the May 3, 2006, issue of the *Atlanta Journal Constitution* indicated that in Mississippi's coastal counties of Hancock, Harrison, and Jackson, 64,210 homes were completely destroyed; 35,320 sustained heavy damage; and 42,306 sustained minor damage.

For the most part, Gulf Coast residents who were able to evacuate before the storms arrived, did so. However, a significant number of people—largely, poor people—stayed because they didn't own vehicles or have other means by which to leave. This, tragically, was the case in New Orleans.

Others stayed because they weren't willing to leave behind pets. This was true especially for elderly people who lived alone with only a beloved pet for companionship. After Katrina, evacuation policies were changed to accommodate pets, as long as they are crated.

David and Elizabeth Goodine live near New Orleans's Ninth Ward, which is home to many of the city's poorest residents. David is pastor of St. Paul's Lutheran Church. Prior to Katrina, Elizabeth was an assistant professor of religious studies at Loyola University, but the school, struggling to recover, declined to renew her contract after the storm. When Katrina hit, the Goodines chose to stay, even though they had the means to leave.

Never have I seen Christ in action so clearly as in the week following Katrina. My husband and I made the decision not to evacuate the city. We stuck with that decision even after the order for mandatory evacuation came across the news late Saturday night. We did it not because we were heroes (far from it!), but because we and a few other members of our church and community knew there were many in our neighborhood, some poor and elderly, who, for various reasons, had been unable to leave. My husband is pastor at St. Paul Lutheran Church in the Marigny, a neighborhood close to the French Quarter that sits on relatively high ground. The church has never flooded and so we reasoned that in the event that the "Big One" really did hit, it might become necessary to open up the building as a shelter.

Well, of course the "Big One" did hit, and in the week that followed, we found ourselves living in the church, along with about fifty other members and neighbors. The church property became "Camp Marigny," a base from which to minister to the ever-growing stream of flood victims rushing up from the horror that the Ninth Ward had become.

On the day the levees breached, we could look down the block from the church and see the water rising. Eventually, it slowed and came no further, but the stream of evacuees did not stop. For days, tired and emotionally distraught, dragging children and old people, they came through our neighborhood on their way to the Superdome and the Convention Center. We watched rescuers pick them up in boats and drop them where the water stopped—that was our neighborhood, the top of the Ninth Ward.

There was a short period of perhaps a day after Katrina ceased brutalizing the coast when it seemed that New Orleans had been spared the worst and that recovery could begin quite quickly. Such hope was dashed when the levees that held back Lake Pontchartrain gave way in three places. Since much of

New Orleans is below sea level, filthy, contaminated water gushed through the breached levees, eventually inundating eighty percent of the city with depths of up to twenty feet. Those who survived the hurricane now found themselves struggling to escape surging floodwaters. Many fled to their attics. As the water continued to rise, those who had the tools to do so cut holes in attic ceilings and climbed onto their rooftops to await rescue. Others, lacking tools or strength, drowned in their own homes. In the aftermath of Katrina, more than 1,800 people died, many waiting for help that didn't come, or didn't arrive in time. Months later, many homes still bear spray painted markings, epitaphs of a sort, indicating the number of bodies discovered entombed inside after the waters receded. *1 Dead in Attic*, a book by *New Orleans Times-Picayune* columnist Chris Rose, includes, along with others, the story of Thomas Coleman, a retired longshoreman, who died in the attic of his home on St. Roch Avenue in the Eighth Ward.

Gaby Haze, a nurse consultant and member of Gethsemane Lutheran Church in Chalmette, Louisiana, evacuated with her family and thirty-six group home residents. Gaby recounts how a neighbor's seventy-three-year-old aunt died on the Haze rooftop. "The water came up so fast that by the time they got a life jacket on her, the water was already up to the roof. [Her body] stayed on the roof for weeks. There was a sign on our house noting there was one dead person, and the neighbors thought it was my husband, Kaki, who usually doesn't evacuate. We learned later who it really was."

Not all New Orleans residents waited for help to come to them. Many chose instead to wade through putrid, chest-high floodwaters in search of food, clean water, and shelter. Because the land along the Mississippi River is higher in elevation than other parts of New Orleans, many went toward the Superdome, only to discover new horrors once they arrived. It was complete chaos, with more than 25,000 traumatized people crammed into a facility never intended to be a housing unit. Inside the wind-damaged Superdome, evacuees suffered without electricity, functioning bathrooms, or basic necessities. The heat and humidity were stifling. It was a life-threatening situation, especially for evacuees without access to the daily medications they needed. Six people were confirmed to have died at the Superdome, at least one while sitting in a lawn chair outside the arena. Four more bodies were removed from the Ernest N. Morial Convention Center, where another 20,000 desperate people congregated. Violence erupted, inflicting further pain on lives already ravaged by storm and flood.

It took several days for rescue workers and government authorities to address the crisis at the Superdome. Finally, three days after Katrina's assault on New Orleans, buses rolled in. People were herded onto them like cattle and shipped out of the city. Many wound up in Houston, where mass shelters housed 65,000 desperate people. In the chaos, children were separated from parents and husbands from wives, sometimes ending up in shelters in different cities. Communication was impossible even for those who had cell phones because so many communication towers had been damaged or destroyed.

Soon it became clear that the effects of this natural disaster were bigger and far more devastating than anyone had anticipated. Until the floodwaters receded, normal post-hurricane rescue and relief efforts were stymied. But this wasn't a "normal" catastrophe. Since much of New Orleans is below sea level, and water always flows to the lowest point, there was no place for the floodwaters to go.

The city's infrastructure was in shambles, and those in positions of responsibility were overwhelmed. Things grew more chaotic as local, state, and federal officials got tangled up in their attempts to address the situation. The federal government wasn't fully prepared to respond. City and state governments were in disarray. People were basically left to fend for themselves.

The flood played no favorites, inundating poor and prosperous neighborhoods alike. Many months later, some neighborhoods still look like a war zone. Downed trees and piles of rubble that once were homes stretch on for miles. In others, residents live in FEMA trailers parked in driveways while they muck out and rebuild their homes. New neighborhoods exist today in what were open fields before Katrina. The trailers in these neighborhoods provide shelter for some of the thousands of people made homeless by the devastation.

But the storm destroyed more than real estate. People who had been neighbors for decades now live hundreds of miles apart, without means of visiting one another or, in some cases, of even communicating. People whose own homes suffered little or no damage ended up losing their jobs because their work places were destroyed. Others are unemployed because they no longer have a way to get to and from work. So much was lost—schools, hospitals, libraries, communities—but Katrina's greatest cost was in human lives. Relief workers were still finding corpses eight months after the storm. According to Kevin Massey, assistant director for ELCA Domestic Disaster Response, "Hurricane Katrina created something that many never thought possible in this land—a population of people evacuated and displaced, uprooted and without a home. People who fled the deadly winds and rushing waters of the storm arrived in every state and live now in uncertainty of when, if ever, they can return. The storm laid bare clear lines of social and racial inequality, and many of the people living with scarce resources before the storm are the same ones now left with nothing."

*   *   *   *   *

Scientists have determined that Katrina was a powerful category 3 hurricane when it made its second and third landfalls on the Gulf Coast. As horrific as the damage was in New Orleans, it is one city and provides only part of the story. Bishop Ronald Warren of the Southeastern Synod of the ELCA, which includes Mississippi, Tennessee, Georgia, and Alabama, recalls his first visit to the Mississippi coast just days after the powerful storm hit: "I [was] a trained fire fighter and chaplain on rescue teams in Milwaukee County, Wisconsin, so I knew there would be police and National Guard who would limit access to the area. But by Friday I couldn't wait any more. So we went [to the coast]. It was totally devastated. Miles and miles of foundations, with no houses on them."

Bishop Warren visited Grace Lutheran Church in Long Beach, Mississippi, which is the westernmost congregation in the Southeastern Synod. Grace's pastor, Barb Hunter, and her husband John lost their home to the thirty-two-foot surge caused by Katrina's 160 mph winds. All they found of what used to be their home was a crystal bowl, some CorningWare, two golf clubs, two platters, a stapler, a folding chair, and a ceramic Christmas ornament embossed with an angel that had miraculously survived the winds and waves. Bishop Warren found the Hunters and several others living without electricity in the church building. He got them a generator so they could refrigerate their food.

Generators were also in short supply at the hospital where John Hunter was working as a nurse. After the storm, area hospital staffs labored in stifling heat, delivering babies and doing surgery by flashlight so that generators could provide the power needed to sustain patients on life support and run other basic equipment. "In spite of extremely difficult challenges, they actually did a wonderful job of feeding everyone, including the staff, three hot meals a day and doing enormous amounts of triage work as people arrived with injuries from debris and from floating around in toxic water for hours," Pastor Hunter recounts.

On Sunday, six days after Katrina, Bishop Warren and Pastor Hunter led worship together in the sanctuary of Grace Lutheran Church. Later that same day, while Methodists worshiped in the sanctuary, Episcopalians gathered in Grace's fellowship hall amidst boxes of relief supplies that had begun pouring in shortly after the storm. The focal point of this unusual worship space was a makeshift altar, on which sat a statue of the Virgin Mary. Picking up the statue, the Episcopal priest presiding over the service announced to those assembled, "This is all we found from what was left of St. Patrick's [Episcopal Church]. But, as we all learned as children, the church is not a building. [The church] is the people, and the church is going to rebuild."

*   *   *   *   *

It's impossible to grasp the magnitude and the complexity of the loss caused by Katrina. Though the storm caused only minor damage to the home of Dr. David and Carole Neubauer of Slidell, Louisiana, Dr. Neubauer was unable to return to his University of New Orleans office for a semester and never did get phone service in his office before he retired in May 2006. Many of their friends didn't fare as well. Dr. Neubauer admits, "I'm wondering how to respond to this," and his wife Carole adds, "Everything is different now. I think I may have survivor's guilt. Why were we spared and so many, many people we know weren't? For a while we would leave and come back. Then for a while we didn't want to leave because it was too hard to come back into it."

Grace Lutheran Church in New Orleans sustained eight feet of water and had to be gutted to the studs. For seven and a half months, a remnant of the congregation worshiped in a local funeral home, returning to the church building for the first time on Easter Sunday, April 15, 2006. Although things are going well enough, Pastor Duke grieves for what was. "I was called to serve a Grace Lutheran that is very different than the one that exists now," he says. "Grace is averaging about sixty-five percent of its pre-Katrina attendance."

While some grieved for what they had been, others lamented losing what might have been. In January 2005, a new social services agency called Lutheran Episcopal Services of Mississippi (LESM) was formed as a direct result of the ELCA full communion agreement with the Episcopal Church USA. The impact of the disaster on the young agency was huge. As of April 1, 2006, LESM began restructuring its recovery and rebuilding efforts with Lutheran Social Services of the South (LSSS) under the direction of Lutheran Disaster Response. At the same time, LESM continues to be grateful for its Episcopal partners as they work together as Lutheran Episcopal Services of Mississippi with Katrina Aid Today. Katrina Aid Today is a national case management consortium funded by a grant monitored by the Department of Homeland Security's Federal Emergency Management Agency. Donations to support the program came from the international community.

*   *   *   *   *

Although Peggy Contos-Hahn lives in Houston, she experienced loss on both a personal and professional level because of the storm. As assistant to the bishop of the Texas–Louisiana Synod of the ELCA, Contos-Hahn was called upon to help coordinate the initial disaster response efforts, and she also opened her home to four generations of her own family. She recalls her family's heart-wrenching decision to leave New Orleans:

"I couldn't stop the tears when my mom called at 7:00 a.m., August 29, 2005, to say, 'Peggy, we are coming your way right now.' I had begged my parents to leave [New Orleans], but I understood why they resisted. My grandpa was in critical condition in East Jefferson Hospital, and [if they evacuated] he would have to be left behind, to end his life without his family around him. 'I have a responsibility to life' was my dad's only comment."

She recalls a scripture passage from Matthew 28, "I am with you always, to the end of the age" (v. 20), and observes, "My grandpa was not dying alone."

Peggy Contos-Hahn's grandfather died two days later and was buried ten days after that in a temporary grave in Lafayette, Louisiana. Approximately a month after Katrina, Peggy and her family returned to his home for the first time. "I am glad my grandpa didn't see his home. 'Dust to dust' was my main thought as we pried open dressers that were swollen with water still filling the drawers. [We] carried the nauseating refrigerator to the curb. We went room to room. The mold was already growing everywhere. Definitely one of the saddest things I've ever done— yet seemed oddly right that the stuff left when he did. It felt like looking directly into the face of death."

But Contos-Hahn sees Easter hope. "People will rebuild. It's what we are wired to do. Some are going back, making order out of the mess. Others will never go back; they will start their life in a new place. I see the heaviness in their eyes—a deeper sort of maturity. Even in the youth and children. But I also see the hope. They have seen the force of nature, the worst of people and the best of people. The face of death and the face of God, known as Katrina.

"My son Matt reminded me of my favorite Bible verse: 'We have this hope, a sure and steadfast anchor of the soul, a hope that enters the inner shrine behind the curtain, where Jesus, a forerunner on our behalf, has entered' (Hebrews 6:19-20).

"The anchor holds us tight."

Discussion questions

1. Where were you when you learned about the destruction caused by the hurricanes and flooding?
2. What is the worst natural disaster you have experienced personally?
3. What are some of the storms you've weathered in your own life?
4. What evidence of God's presence have you experienced following losses in your life?
5. Who or what has sustained you in your losses?

Reflection starters

Select one of the following scripture passages: Psalm 46; Genesis 8:1-14; Mark 4:35-41; or John 14:23-27.

1. If you are alone, read the passage slowly three times. Then choose a particular word or phrase within the passage. Close your eyes and focus on that word or phrase for several minutes. Share your thoughts with God in prayer.

2. If you are with a group of people, have someone read the scripture passage aloud. Take a couple moments to reflect silently on what you've heard. Then read aloud the passage again and invite group members to select a particular word or phrase that captures their attention. Read the passage aloud a third time and invite group members to share personal reflections on the passage. Close with a prayer, inviting each person to add a petition if he or she chooses.

Action items

Here are some things you can do to prepare for emergencies.

1. Make a list of names, addresses, and phone numbers of people you will need to contact in an emergency. Keep copies in your purse or wallet, as well as next to your phone and in your vehicle.

2. Make a plan for where you would go and how you would get there in the event that you need to evacuate.

3. Prepare an emergency kit of basic supplies, as well as a list of things you will need if you have to leave your home in a hurry.

4. Make a list of all account numbers and passwords. Give a copy of the list to someone whom you trust but who does

not live with you. If your list is lost, you will have access to another.

5. Talk with others about what they have done to prepare for an emergency.

2

Rescue and Exile:
The Body of Christ Is Wounded

"O LORD, God of my salvation, when, at night, I cry out
in your presence, let my prayer come before you; incline
your ear to my cry. For my soul is full of troubles, and my
life draws near to Sheol. I am counted among those who
go down to the Pit; I am like those who have no help, like
those forsaken among the dead, like the slain that lie in the
grave, like those whom you remember no more, for they are
cut off from your hand."
—Psalm 88:1-5

Katrina, and later Rita, brought us face to face with our
vulnerability and our finiteness. As inhabitants of the Gulf
Coast, we had been through storms before and not only had
survived, but had come out of them pretty much unharmed.
We knew the routine: board up our homes, pack a few
necessities, and make the slow commute north to Monroe,
Shreveport, and Dallas; northeast to Jackson and Memphis;
west to Baton Rouge, Lafayette, and Houston. We headed out,
hoping that the fury of this storm would be minimal and our
return home imminent.

But no previous storm had packed the punch of Katrina.

From the safety of distance, we watched a powerful force uncoil her vengeance. A day later, we watched with the rest of the nation while raging water swallowed up New Orleans and the surrounding area. There was no escaping the gravity of the situation when televisions showed people standing on the roofs of their houses with signs pleading to be rescued. The "Big One" had hit. This time we weren't going to escape unscathed, and we surely weren't going home anytime soon.

While we struggled to come to grips with this new reality, the communities to which we had relocated momentarily started gearing up to provide for our needs over the long haul. Thousands had evacuated to Baton Rouge, about an hour's drive west of New Orleans in normal traffic. More would arrive soon, essentially doubling the city's population overnight. Additional emergency shelters were hastily opened, and when they couldn't accommodate the need, Baton Rouge residents opened their homes.

A survey conducted by the sociology department of Louisiana State University (LSU) discovered that fifty percent of Baton Rouge households provided shelter for evacuees during Katrina, and more than sixty percent volunteered in one way or another to assist with relief efforts after the storm. (Research results from www.lsu.edu, link to the sociology department.)

Months after Katrina, many "temporary residents" continue to live in Baton Rouge with family and friends. Some commute across the congested interstate to New Orleans where they have jobs, but no place to live. This has created new ministry challenges and opportunities. Dr. Walton Ehrhardt, a licensed professional counselor who lost his private practice in the storm, now works with the ELCA Texas–Louisiana Gulf Coast Synod, helping displaced families deal with the spiritual and emotional trauma caused by the double whammy of hurricanes Katrina and Rita. Dr. Ehrhardt has dubbed this the "Kat-Rita Effect."

"Depression and anxiety are the disorders of the day," says Ehrhardt. He acknowledges that people are frustrated with FEMA, insurance companies, the Corps of Engineers, and government in general. According to Ehrhardt, "Tempers are short."

Ehrhardt has worked with 450 families who still are displaced eight months after the storms. While many live with family in the area, others are not so fortunate. Because of a shortage of workers and layers of bureaucracy, families live in the upper levels of ruined houses, without air conditioning or heat. One couple lived for three months in the stall of a horse barn after their houseboat rode the storm surge seven miles inland.

Ehrhardt counsels with many elderly people, including a woman who watched her two beloved companion dogs drown while she waited in water over her head for three days and nights to be rescued. Others without mortgage or flood insurance have asked, "Pastor Walt, is it sinful to want to die?" They tell him that they are too old to start over. "And then they begin again, on a new day." Ehrhardt adds, "Every day is a new day!"

Pastor John McCullough-Bade, on permanent disability from Parkinson's disease, is writing and composing video pieces to help tell the Katrina story. He has found that, since Katrina, ministry frequently happens out in the community in places like the grocery store.

All it takes these days is a simple question while waiting in line at the store—a line that has lengthened exponentially since August 29. "How did you fare in the storm?" Or perhaps it takes a keen eye to notice the New Orleans car dealer's logo on the car in front of you at the gas station. Or an ear tuned to a certain nuance of voice that suggests a New Orleans address.

[I]t doesn't take much to initiate the telling of the story. It's as if the fragile levee holding in the emotions and agony of the past days is breached, and the floodwaters of words, tears, and emotions come rushing forth.

"I lost my house, my belongings, my car, everything."

"My brother and his family lived down the street from us. And my mom lived a few blocks away. And my sister and her two children a mile farther."

Four families, four houses, fifteen people—all devastated.

"I've had twelve people from New Orleans living with me since the storm. It's been six months!"

"I stayed because my mother had just gotten out of hospital and we thought it would be too hard for her to travel. When the water came, we went to the Superdome. It was as bad as they say...maybe worse. When the buses finally came, we were taken to the Astrodome in Houston. We're trying to get back home, but there's not much home to go back to."

"I had to leave in such a rush that I didn't even have time to grab my Bible. How is a preacher supposed to preach without a Bible?"

The stories can be heard everywhere because the loss is everywhere. As we listen as people of faith, we bear witness to these stories. And we also bear witness and connect these stories to the greater . . . story of a God who enters into the pain of life, who walks the road of the cross, who knows God-forsaken-ness and loss. [This God] also fashioned life out of death and hope out of despair. That is the truth that makes the story gospel.

The story—of Katrina and its aftermath—is being told and lived. And *the* story—the God story of death and new life, of cross and resurrection—is being told and lived, as well. All we need to do is ask, and look, and listen.

In Houston, city leaders literally worked overnight to put in place the world's largest welcome mat. Mayor Bill White and Harris County Judge Robert Eckels converted both the Reliant Center south of downtown and the downtown George R. Brown Convention Center into massive shelters and command centers to coordinate the arrival of nearly 300,000 people, many of whom endured a six-hour bus trip from New Orleans after spending several horrific days in sub-human conditions in the Louisiana Superdome. Initially it was thought the Astrodome would house the 25,000 people stranded in the Superdome. However, the two mass shelter sites housed a total of 65,000 for several weeks until other arrangements could be made for them. The Red Cross opened thirty additional shelters in and around Harris County. Many churches threw open their doors to accept and care for evacuees, and private citizens, with hearts to help, took complete strangers into their homes, not knowing how long they would stay. It was amazing how quickly a city of four million people came together to welcome the influx of people. In a matter of days, a system was in place to provide shelter, food, medical care, and communication services for thousands of people, many of whom had become separated from family members in all the chaos.

Elliot Gershenson, executive director of Interfaith Ministries of Greater Houston, was one of several community leaders tapped by Mayor Bill White to devise and implement a plan to feed the thousands who now inhabited the massive shelters. "[Interfaith Ministries] committed to raising the money and finding volunteers to serve the food, Second Baptist [served by Pastor Ed Young] scheduled the volunteers in shifts," reports Gershenson. "Thirty thousand people came to food handling and orientation sessions Saturday and Sunday of Labor Day weekend. Another 12,000 came the next three days . . . volunteers served three meals a day for eighteen days."

More than $4.5 million was raised in less than a week to cover the costs of the food and other items evacuees needed immediately. Gershenson estimates that 100,000 volunteers were involved in one way or another in Operation Compassion and other volunteer efforts, and he knows that some people took time away from their jobs for a few weeks in order to help. Houston's Muslim community turned out 2,500 strong to serve meals on September 11, 2005, and Muslim doctors, eager to be part of the response, also helped set up mobile clinics to provide much-needed medical care for evacuees.

Fred and Kay Wasden were in the midst of a corporate transfer from New Orleans to Houston when Katrina hit. They had sold their home along the Seventeenth Street Canal south of Lake Pontchartrain, but the deal wasn't yet closed. The Wasdens evacuated to Houston two days before Katrina made landfall. Late Monday evening, August 29, they learned via the Internet that the water at an intersection near their New Orleans home was eight feet deep. Kay Wasden describes the generous treatment that they received in a community that wasn't their home quite yet.

Shell Oil Company (Fred's employer) went to work getting apartments for all their people. We moved into one the following Sunday. They contacted everyone they could reach and told them to come to Houston.

That Thursday and Friday, I went shopping. We needed everything. On Friday, my husband and I [drove] by Social Services, and saw a huge crowd of desperate people in the parking lot, just standing around. They were stunned and dazed. Not knowing what [else] to do, we asked them what they needed, and then [we] went and bought it and brought it back to them—ice, food, drink, formula.

[We were] offered a spot for our two-year-old, Ben, in a local Methodist preschool. They took in children from seven New Orleans families and didn't charge us any fees. They had a pre-printed shopping list of basic things we might need. I could just circle what I needed, or add things to it. The next day, when I dropped my son off at school, they [gave] me the things I needed.

Like many evacuees, the Wasdens received gift cards to all sorts of retail stores. Knowing that so many of their New Orleans neighbors had lost everything and had no flood insurance to help finance rebuilding, the Wasdens tried to share the gifts with them but often met resistance. According to Kay, "[T]hey were so proud. Even though they had incredible needs, they didn't want to take any of the gift cards from us because we had also lost a great deal. I would tell them the cards were a gift from a church, and then they'd accept them."

*   *   *   *   *

When it became evident that Hurricane Katrina was likely headed for the Louisiana coast and that the city of New Orleans was directly in its path, staff in the Texas–Louisiana Gulf Coast Synod office began calling pastors to ask about their plans and preparations. After the storm passed, we spent several days trying to reconnect with our leaders. Slowly but surely, we learned their whereabouts—Jackson, Atlanta, Houston, somewhere in Tennessee, with family in Dallas, Shreveport, Lafayette, Baton Rouge. All were safe. Praise God! We asked them about their flocks. They had located some, but not all. They would keep trying. We asked them to keep us informed.

Immediately after Katrina blew out of the area, as bishop of the Texas–Louisiana Gulf Coast Synod, I wrote a letter to my colleagues in the Conference of Bishops of the ELCA, giving them a snapshot of each of our congregations in southern Louisiana. I provided them with information about our pastors and associates in ministry, and the congregations they served. I asked them to invite congregations in their synods to partner with our churches. I also appealed to my colleagues to hold an ingathering of funds to provide financial support for congregational leaders whose churches would not be able to meet their financial commitments for the foreseeable future. I indicated that I would be using the Bishop's Discretionary Fund to allow leaders to access emergency funds without having to go through a lot of red tape. I felt comfortable doing so since I knew them all personally.

The response to my request was immediate and overwhelming. Our office phones began ringing with pledges of support from congregations and individuals throughout the United States and the Caribbean. Letters with checks attached poured into the synod office. To a person, the letter writers assured us that they were praying for us. Friends, acquaintances, former classmates, and parishioners sent financial support designated to particular church leaders and congregations. Delivering these gifts presented something of a dilemma, however, since there wasn't any mail service in New Orleans or the surrounding area, and few people were there anyway. Once we located our leaders, we solved the problem by asking them to provide routing and checking account numbers so we could wire the money directly to their accounts. This process continued for about three weeks.

The generosity of people's hearts touched our hearts greatly. We received gifts ranging from just a few dollars to hundreds of thousands of dollars. Many $500 to $1,000 gifts came in the form of personal checks from compassionate individuals and families. People on fixed incomes with little to spare sent gifts because they wanted to help. Students devised creative ways to raise money and have fun doing it. The letters accompanying their gifts lifted our spirits more than words can express.

Following a children's sermon based on the parable of the talents (Matthew 25:14-30), children at Mount Cross Lutheran Church in Camarillo, California were given $5 bills and given three choices: spend the money on themselves, save the money and return it later, or invest the money. A month later, the children returned with envelopes bulging with money and stories of how they had enlisted friends, relatives, and their parent's coworkers into helping them with money-making projects. In one month, twenty children grew the original $200 into a $1,200 gift for disaster relief.

A few weeks after Katrina, I flew to Minnesota to attend a meeting at the Minneapolis Area Synod offices. I learned from Bishop Craig Johnson that congregations of the Minneapolis Area Synod had held a special ingathering of funds to support relief and recovery work on the Gulf Coast. (The Minneapolis Area and Texas–Louisiana Gulf Coast synods are ELCA partner synods.) I was stunned when Bishop Johnson presented a check for $200,000.

Some gifts came with history attached. The Staten Island Conference of the Metropolitan New York Synod explained that following the terrorist attacks on New York City in 2001, the synod was gifted with a sum of money to bring aid and comfort to the people of the island who were directly affected by loss of income from the destruction of the Towers. They wanted to honor that gift by helping others in need during this natural disaster.

Gifts continue to come—from Maui where children took up a "noisy offering" of loose change, to a New Jersey congregation that partnered with a church camp in Texas to provide two VBS programs for congregations in New Orleans. They remind us that during this long period of recovery, we are not alone. The body of Christ walks with us.

The importance of the body of Christ was echoed by Andrew Genszler, director of domestic policy in the ELCA's Washington office, a position he assumed just two weeks following Katrina.

I started [in] this position knowing that disaster recovery would be a major focus as we're trying to formulate a response that is helpful. We've been trying to wait out the finger pointing to develop a plan for federal policy that will be helpful, given what ELCA survivors, leaders, and workers are telling us along the Gulf Coast.

Personally, I am involved because I am part of the body of Christ. Even though I'm a Midwesterner . . . and do not know a lot about the area, as part of the body of Christ, I am compelled to act on behalf of people I've never met. The body of Christ connects us beyond the battles about budgets and how we should proceed with the recovery effort. We are a church bound together in the new Body of Christ with service, reconciliation, and hospitality as defining marks.

*   *   *   *   *

It's painful and difficult to adjust when the routines and activities that provide stability in our lives are ripped away. The evacuation of the Gulf Coast was an Exodus experience—a crossing not of the Red Sea, but of the Sabine Pass, the border between Louisiana and Texas. Many who made the journey had never before traveled outside the city limits of New Orleans. Mingled with their fear and uncertainty was a strong faith in God's presence with them and care for them.

They left bearing few, if any, belongings, forced to flee their homes by a combination of forces over which they had no control—nature, weakened levees, raging water, and failures of leadership.

Months later, thousands remain in exile in a "foreign land." They struggle to navigate their way through the complex process involved in replacing cars destroyed in the flood or acquiring permits and building materials to repair damaged homes. For some, the documents they need in order to return home or to start life over again in a new place are gone forever—carried away by wind or water.

Loss always elicits grief, which finds expression in a variety of emotions. First, shock, disbelief, bewilderment. Next, denial. Then anger, which, if internalized rather than directed toward something constructive outside of ourselves, will ultimately lead to despair.

For people of sorrow, the psalmist's words carry personal meaning: "I am utterly bowed down and prostrate; all day long I go around mourning. . . . I am utterly spent and crushed; I groan because of the tumult of my heart. O Lord, all my longing is known to you; my sighing is not hidden from you. My heart throbs, my strength fails me; as for the light of my eyes—it also has gone from me. . . . But it is for you, O LORD, that I wait; it is you, O Lord my God, who will answer" (Psalm 38:6, 8-10, 15).

Discussion questions

1. What losses have you experienced in your life?
2. When have you been dependent on others?
3. We often don't allow enough time for people to grieve and adjust to their new realities. What have you learned about your own grieving process through your losses?
4. What has surprised you about the responses of people you've tried to support through a time of loss and grief?
5. What has surprised you about how you've adjusted to changes in your own life?
6. Grief and loss are part of life. What resources do your church or community provide to help people who are grieving?

Reflection starters

Reflect on one of the following psalms, using the suggestions for reflection included in chapter 1 (see page 28).

Psalm 23—The Lord is my Shepherd.

Psalm 27—The Lord is my light and salvation.

Psalm 30—Weeping may remain for a night, but joy comes in the morning.

Psalm 38—Come quickly to help me, O Lord.

Psalm 70—You are my help and my deliverer.

Action items

1. *Interdependent circles.* There are times when we will all need help adjusting to some situations. Perhaps we experience a major illness, a death of a loved one, a stalled car, or a fire or flood. There also are times when others are counting on us to help them. List the people to whom you would turn first if suddenly you found you couldn't manage for yourself for some reason. Make a second list of people you'd be willing to assist at any hour of the day or night if they were in trouble.

2. *Prayer in action.* Establish a personal resource library of movies, books, pamphlets, articles, poems, and other items that have been helpful and meaningful to you during your times of challenge and change. You may want to get duplicate copies of some of your favorites to have on hand to lend or give to others who face difficult times.

3

Relief and Grief:

The Body of Christ
Is a Wounded Healer

"God is our refuge and strength, a very present help in
trouble. Therefore we will not fear, though the earth should
change, though the mountains shake in the heart of the
sea; though its waters roar and foam, though the mountains
tremble with its tumult. . . . The LORD of hosts is with us;
the God of Jacob is our refuge. . . . 'Be still, and know that
I am God! I am exalted among the nations, I am exalted in
the earth.' The LORD of hosts is with us; the God of Jacob is
our refuge."
—Psalm 46:1-3, 7, 10-11

Storms!
There are storms that hit full force, unleashing the awe-
some power of nature upon people and property.
Storms!
There are storms—metaphors for events in our lives—
whose power rivals that of nature to catch us off guard and to
disturb—even destroy—our sense of security and well-being.

Storms are powerful reminders of how little in life we actually determine or control.

Two storms—hurricanes—whipped up other storms. Hundreds of thousands of people survived the onslaught of nature only to feel themselves being sucked into misery, depression, and despair in the horrific aftermath of the storms.

*   *   *   *   *

A couple of weeks after Katrina, I arranged to meet pastors from the greater New Orleans area for food, fellowship, and conversation at a restaurant in Baton Rouge. Since flights were limited and no seats were available, I secured the services of Angel Flight pilots to get to Baton Rouge. Pastor John McCullough-Bade picked me up at the airport, and we drove together to First Lutheran Church and then to the restaurant. A trip that normally takes about ten minutes took well over half an hour. The marked increase in traffic was due to the fact that the city's population had more than doubled since the storm.

Although a number of pastors from the hardest hit areas weren't able to join us, it was good to be together and to hear, firsthand, how things were going for them. It was clear that many were struggling to figure out what their roles would be in the immediate and long-term aftermath of Katrina. They talked about the tremendous influx of evacuees and their feelings of helplessness because they weren't able to do more to assist them. All had experienced the storm's impact in one way or another, and I could see that they were struggling mightily to deal with their losses.

Toward the end of the conversation, frustration began to surface with regard to the church's response to the disaster, including that of Lutheran Disaster Response. LDR's commitment is to work with survivors throughout the entire recovery and rebuilding process, so its efforts were not, perhaps, as evident initially as those of first-responders like the Red Cross and Salvation Army. Another dilemma for leaders of ELCA congregations in Louisiana and Mississippi is that there are no judicatory offices close by. While other denominations with a greater presence in the area have church leaders living nearby, our judicatory offices are located in another state altogether. I understand, however, that these explanations could provide only a little consolation in the face of so much loss.

Reminders of what has been lost are everywhere in New Orleans. Restaurants lack the staff to keep regular hours. Trash pick-up is sporadic. Street signs are missing. Volunteers from outside the city provide medical care at temporary church clinics. Tents and FEMA trailers dot the landscape. Blue tarps and sheets of plywood mark damaged roofs and missing windows. Church fellowship halls are lined with air mattresses and cots to accommodate volunteer workers. It's impossible not to feel strong emotion in the face of such loss. Healing happens slowly over time, with setbacks and, perhaps, flashbacks along the way. The road to recovery is a wild ride, and our hearts cry out for help.

Healer of our ev'ry ill, light of each tomorrow,
give us peace beyond our fear, and hope beyond our sorrow.

You who know our fears and sadness,
grace us with your peace and gladness;
Spirit of all comfort, fill our hearts.

In the pain and joy beholding
how your grace is still unfolding,
give us all your vision, God of love.

Give us strength to love each other,
ev'ry sister, ev'ry brother;
Spirit of all kindness, be our guide.

You who know each thought and feeling,
teach us all your way of healing;
Spirit of compassion, fill each heart.
—"Healer of Our Every Ill" by Marty Haugen

During times of trouble, people typically turn to the church for consolation and support. But what happens when the church itself is wounded? What happens when the patient must also serve as doctor? Katrina and the ensuing flood wrecked havoc on churches, destroying buildings and scattering members. Congregations in the Texas–Louisiana Gulf Coast Synod saw their memberships reduced by fifty percent or more as members evacuated and then found it impossible to return. For Pastor Patrick Keen who serves Bethlehem Lutheran Church in New Orleans, trying to rebuild the facility while holding together a congregation in diaspora has given new meaning to outreach ministry. Pastor Keen relates:

We are slowly moving, but we are moving. We're about ninety percent done with the interior. There's still a lot of work to do on the exterior. The sanctuary hadn't been painted in fifteen years. The kitchen and bathrooms had not really had anything done in the forty years they've been here. But we've got that entire pretty well redone now.

We've been housing groups at the church who are working at Grace [Lutheran in New Orleans] and here. We've been feeding them as a congregation, providing breakfast. When they're working here, we give them lunch. And we make sure they have dinner somewhere.

We have about thirty percent of our people back—the ones who were homeowners. Those who were renters cannot afford to come back. There's a lot of price gouging going on and rental property is really hard to come by. So the rest of our folks are scattered with about twenty percent of them in Houston, maybe thirty percent in Atlanta, another thirty percent in Baton Rouge, and the rest everywhere with family and friends. I stay in touch with them, but it's hard and they're going to be out of New Orleans for at least the next year. It's very hard for them to rent where they are too. Most of them lost jobs, and rent in the cities . . . is high also. I focus on linking them up with resources. One great advantage to being part of this Lutheran community is that we have congregations and resources all across the country that we can access. As we are blessed with gift cards, we send these to our members who are not here. Some need transportation and we try to help. We have one long-time member who now lives on the far side of Baton Rouge. He comes in every Sunday and picks people up along the way. It's a two hour trip each way for him.

My vision is that this congregation's proud past gives us the vision we need for the future. If we can get past this current hurricane season, both Bethlehem and New Orleans are going to bounce back. We have to anticipate that we'll have a storm like this every forty or so years and learn how to respond to it right. I anticipate this community of God becoming involved in a housing development project.

Such a project would make good use of Pastor Keen's background. Prior to becoming a pastor he was Director of Habitat for Humanity in Chicago. But first the people have to finish the massive clean-up efforts.

Pastor Keen admits he's concerned that funding to complete the challenge could dry up. "We were counting on [gifts to disaster relief efforts] to cover salaries. I have a vision of the 200 Club: Find 200 people who will commit $200/month for the next three years. That will stabilize us and then we can also extend out to start another mission in the area."

The grassroots response to aid recovery and rebuilding has been both touching and astonishing. We who are on the receiving end of recovery assistance have been blessed over and over again by the hard work and gentle care provided by volunteers from far and near. Bernard Scrogin, LDR state coordinator for Texas and Western Louisiana, has immense gratitude for how volunteers responded in the aftermath of Hurricane Rita. By the end of April, seventy-eight Lutherans from five states had worked to remove debris, rehab, and re-roof seven homes.

"Thank you; thank you; thank you for the help you have given as LSSS/LDR seeks to make a difference in the lives of people adversely affected by Rita," writes Scrogin. "Lutherans in the Golden Triangle [an area of several communities that straddle the Sabine River between Texas and Louisiana] have been very generous in their support. When we asked for tools, you provided in abundance. When we asked for hospitality for volunteers, you again responded."

The synod continues to receive inquiries from folks as far away as Alaska and Hawaii who want to know what their church or community can do. We've learned that volunteers often go home feeling that they received as much or more from the experience as they gave. This was true for a group from Messiah Lutheran Church in Vancouver, Washington, who came to New Orleans in fall 2005 and worked with members of Gethsemane Lutheran Church in Chalmette. When Messiah member Robbie Schmalenberger was asked what most impressed her about the experience, she spoke of the resilience heard in the voices of those who had lost so much.

[These people] were reordering their lives. It was infectious and caused us to think about our own lives and priorities. As we worked together, both as a team and side by side with the families, I had a growing feeling of well-being and even fun. That, too, gave me pause; it seemed incongruous and somehow out of place. But as I observed the families when we were together socially, I sensed that they, too, were enjoying being with us; this was God healing through community. Our physical labor, albeit important, was a vehicle for something even greater. We felt God in action and now have a new sense of God at work in us, through us, for us, and for others.

Flood damage to Gethsemane was extensive, and the congregation's needs were great. When Emmanuel Lutheran Church in Groton, South Dakota, asked how they could help, the synod paired the two congregations. Emmanuel sent a monetary gift shortly after the hurricanes but felt the push to do more. And more they did. Emmanuel members Renee and Bob Swisher talked to Pastor Elizabeth Johnson about a plan to fill a horse trailer with supplies and deliver them to Louisiana. The idea "grew feet" when they decided to expand the plan beyond Emmanuel to include the entire community of 1,300 people. For three weeks, monetary donations, clothing, shoes, food, school supplies, and toys were collected at Groten Area Elementary School, virtually filling the main hallway with generosity. There was even an organ to replace Gethsemane's instrument, which was lost in the flood.

On February 6, 2006, Bob Swisher and his good friend, Craig Jondahl, drove straight through from Groton, South Dakota, to Chalmette, Louisiana, to deliver the gifts. Craig's aunt, Marcia LaMarche, a long-time resident of Lafayette, helped guide them through the tangled streets on the final leg of their 1,500-mile journey, and Gethsemane deacon, Mike Perez, welcomed them warmly and helped them unload the precious cargo. The next day, Bob and Craig drove to Lafayette, Louisiana, to deliver boxes of medical supplies, donated by a church in Sioux Falls, South Dakota, to a free clinic serving victims of Hurricane Katrina to the east and Hurricane Rita to the west.

Back home in Groton, Pastor Elizabeth Johnson reflects:

> We as a congregation received more from Gethsemane Lutheran and their fellow mission outposts. Their attitude, their spirits throughout this year have inspired us. God in the midst of the raging waters? God was right there. Is still. We add or added little. We but responded to God's unfailing presence. For he dwells in the heart of a faithful multitude, who just . . . happens to live along the Gulf.

My prayer is that we do not forget. We so easily move from one day to the next, from one fad or fury, one news craze to the next news twist. But may our little ones especially . . . may we help them remember that someone was in need. Someone in our own backyard needed help. And by the power of the Spirit we were able to help. God has blessed us and continues to bless us, but so that we may be a blessing to others. Someone was in need. Someone is still in need. And we *can* help. In faith we *can* make a difference.

God's people have made a difference and will continue to do so for as long as it takes to rebuild property and lives destroyed by the storms and flood. While most volunteers spend a day or two, or a week or two, making a difference, some rearrange their lives to respond over the long haul. Daryl Daugs, a retired pastor and former social worker from Gig Harbor, Washington, came south to check out the situation and ended up staying for more than six months. For much of that time, Daryl served as the site coordinator at a volunteer camp set up at Hosanna Lutheran Church in Mandeville, Louisiana, where many volunteers working in the flooded areas south of Lake Pontchartrain were housed and fed.

Another retired pastor, Phil Blom, has both a heart to help and valuable experience to offer. "My story begins with the flood [and] fire [in] Grand Forks, North Dakota, in 1997, which flooded eighty percent of our city," says Blom. "Our home was flooded, my parents' home was flooded, my sisters' homes were flooded, our church was flooded, and my wife's school was flooded.

"Our lifeline that we held on to—or that held us [was this promise from] 1 Peter 5:10—'after you have suffered for a little while . . . Christ will himself restore, support, strengthen, and establish you.' We didn't know how or when [that would happen], but we held on, believing . . . and then came the body of Christ that lifted us slowly out of the muck. Remembering those blessings prompted [my wife], Sue, and I to say we needed to be a blessing when this . . . disaster . . . took place."

Phil had intended originally to come for a couple of months, but his ministry has meant so much to so many that now he's coming down for weeks at a time on a semi-regular basis. He has involved others, too, including his brother Dave who spent his vacation mucking out houses in New Orleans. Money from the Blom Memorial for Missions, a fund established by the Blom family when Phil's parents died, has been designated to help restore several New Orleans churches.

Some who pitch in to help start in one role and continue on in others. This is the case for Amy Brassett who assisted with rescue and relief efforts in Baton Rouge on behalf of the Red Cross. Noting the situation of 500 families now living in Renaissance Village, one of dozens of new FEMA trailer communities, Amy chose to stay when the Red Cross moved on. She now partners with Louisiana Family Recovery Corps to locate resources for the citizens of this makeshift community. Amy has arranged church services, solicited recreational equipment for the children living in small FEMA trailers, and arranged special community events. Currently, she is negotiating for air-conditioned places for people to gather in over the summer, and a locked storage unit to store the many donations she receives for residents.

Volunteers play a vital role in helping individuals, families, and communities recover from disaster. The work they do, the prayers they offer, the support they provide, and the stories they take home and share with others are valuable beyond measure. But arranging food, shelter, transportation, and work experiences for thousands of volunteers isn't easily accomplished, especially when there's a critical shortage of housing and other resources.

Pastor Ron Unger had just accepted a new call to Christ the King in Kenner, Louisiana, when Katrina made landfall. Instead of leading worship in his new parish, he served Holy Communion to fellow evacuees in a motel lobby in Jackson, Mississippi, using a leftover bagel and a plastic Super 8 cup for a chalice. "It was a very strange way to start a new call," Ron admits. "Normally I'd . . . call on people in their homes and get to know them. But most of them aren't in their homes." Since Christ the King sustained very little damage from either storm or flood, the congregation opened its doors to provide office space for the Lutheran Disaster Response staff and a place for volunteers to get a hot shower and a good night's sleep. Neighboring Atonement Lutheran provides meals for the volunteers.

While giving a tour of the facilities at Christ the King, Ron explained his philosophy about the recovery work. "I let the volunteers and the members of the church handle all this," he said, pointing to the sleeping area where volunteers sleep on air mattresses in a large fellowship room. "I concentrate on the things that I can do as a pastor—preach and provide pastoral care."

He's not going to run out of work any time soon.

Dove of Peace Mission camp is located at Peace Lutheran Church, northeast of Lake Pontchartrain in Slidell, Louisiana. Created largely through the efforts of Pastor Barb Simmers, Dove of Peace is now an affiliate of Lutheran

Disaster Response and has a full-time paid employee to coordinate reservations and work projects. Katie Houck is one of hundreds whose career path took a sharp turn after the hurricanes. She came to New Orleans in May 2005 to work as assistant director for student programs for the Women's Studies Liberal Arts College at Tulane University. Three months later she was fleeing Katrina. Much of Tulane University was relocated to Houston for a semester and Katie's job disappeared. Now she is busy coordinating people and projects at Dove of Peace. Volunteers are boarded and fed at no expense, and work materials and tools are also provided for them. The camp can accommodate up to forty volunteers at a time, and plans are underway to build a second building to host forty to fifty more. It is anticipated that volunteer help will be needed in the area for several years to come.

Don and Marion McClarin, former teachers from Bethel, New York, helped Pastor Simmers get the camp going after Katrina, and they spent five months at the volunteer facility. During that time, the McClarins interacted with well over 600 volunteers from 23 states. "We [were] witnesses to acts of kindness and generosity too numerous to mention," they relate of their time at Dove of Peace. "We are humbled by the relationships we [had] during [those] five months."

Even before the McClarins left, another couple, Dave and Martha Messersmith, was on the scene to take over coordination of the volunteer camp. They offer this assessment of the important role volunteers play in the recovery process:

We've helped house and feed individuals and groups from Minnesota, Michigan, Iowa, Wisconsin, South Carolina, Florida, New York State, Southwest Virginia, and Texas, ranging in size from one person to 25-plus and ranging in age from college students to men and women in their late 70s and early 80s. All have made significant "labor contributions" to help rebuild individual homes as well as Peace Lutheran's church facility itself, which was damaged by Katrina. These volunteers are primarily ELCA and LCMS Lutherans, but Presbyterian, Catholic, and Reformed Christian faiths have also been represented.

Given the enormity of the work to be done to muck out and then rebuild many of the 800,000-plus structures affected in Mississippi and Louisiana, it literally will take an army of volunteers coming here for many years to assist folks since the work must be done one house, one church, and one business at a time.

The healing has just begun.

Discussion questions

1. What do you remember about how people around you expressed grief in your childhood?
2. When you feel discouraged and overwhelmed by the circumstances of your life, what do you do? Where do you turn? Who or what helps you get through the dark times?
3. When you encounter someone who has suffered tremendous loss or hardships, how do you respond to them? What inspires you to get involved? What fears might keep you from responding to their pain?

4. What do you think are some of the most important things to remember in a time of loss and devastation?
5. What do you think you might tell your children or grandchildren about the events of 2005?

Reflection starters

Turn to the book of Job for a time of prayerful reflection. The entire book is worth reading. It is a model of what it means to suffer and to attempt to walk with those who suffer. For personal and group reflection, consider these passages:

Job 3:23-26—I have no peace, no quietness.
Job 10:17-19—Why did you bring me out of the womb?
Job 29:2-5—Remember a time when life was better.
Job 19:25-27—I know that my Redeemer lives.

Action items

1. *The Cycles of our Lives.* Grief and loss are part and parcel of life. Draw a life line of major events you've experienced and rank them on the extent to which you experienced them as a blessing or a loss. To do this, draw a line horizontally across the middle of a sheet of paper. Number the line as zero. Mark numbers above this line in increments of 10 up to 50. Mark numbers below this line in increments of -10 to -50. Across the top of the sheet, mark off 10-year increments from your birth to your present age

Write down a word or short phrase to remind you of some of the major events of your life, placing each in the appropriate place to indicate when in your life it happened and the level of blessing or pain it brought you. Most people who do this will see a pattern of what looks like waves from the highs and lows of their lives.

2. *Prayer in action.* You probably know someone who is suffering from some setback. Make a commitment to pray for that person every day for a week or a month. Write a note letting the person know that you are praying for him or her. Mail or personally deliver the note. It matters. It makes a difference.

4

Recovery and Renewal:
The Body of Christ Organizes for Recovery

"The Spirit of the Lord is upon me, because he has anointed me to bring good news to the poor. He has sent me to proclaim release to the captives and recovery of sight to the blind, to let the oppressed go free, to proclaim the year of the Lord's favor."
—Luke 4:18-19

The liturgy for the "Affirmation of Baptism" in *Lutheran Book of Worship* asks those affirming their baptisms:

Do you intend to continue in the covenant God made with you in Holy Baptism:
> to live among God's faithful people,
> to hear his Word and share in his supper,
> to proclaim the good news of God in Christ through word and deed,
> to serve all people, following the example of our Lord Jesus,
> and to strive for justice and peace in all the earth?"
> (*LBW*, p. 201)

In the fall of 2005, the people of God answered that question with a resounding yes, proclaiming through their words and deeds the good news that God's will to save is stronger than the power of wind and water to destroy. The people of God waded into the muck and pain to serve those in need. Following Jesus' example, they ignored social, economic, political, and religious boundaries to reach out with compassion to all people.

When storms assail us, it is natural to ask, "Where is God in all of this?" Following Katrina and then Rita, God's presence was revealed, as it always is, in the body of Christ.

Lutherans have a strong history of networking with other nonprofit and faith communities to coordinate efforts during and after a disaster to assure that in addition to the initial spontaneous outpouring of help that individuals can, and do, offer, there is structure in place to provide for continued assistance for as long as recovery takes. Lutheran Disaster Response (LDR), a cooperative effort of the Evangelical Lutheran Church in America and the Lutheran Church–Missouri Synod, and Lutheran Social Services of the South (LSSS) are leaders in providing for recovery needs over the long haul.

Heather Feltman, executive director of Lutheran Disaster Response (LDR), says, "An image of our disaster recovery program is . . . a rubber band that expands and contracts as the situation warrants. Hurricane Katrina was a devastating storm on many levels. The rubber band is stretched!" Feltman says that in addition to the destruction caused by the storms, the magnitude of Katrina and Rita created an underlying fear regarding the storms' future impact.

As human beings we fear many things. In a disaster context we fear we may not be able to rebuild our church, our community, or our homes. Many church leaders fear loss of church membership and a loss of benevolence dollars to sustain ministries. The past two years have seen the most devastating disasters we've ever witnessed. This leads to fear of all the changes that we must face—the loss of what was familiar, known, and comfortable. In the midst of such change and living into a new reality, this church's response is unprecedented. In 2005, $55 million was gifted for the ELCA's three relief ministries—international disaster, domestic disaster, and world hunger. The ELCA World Hunger Appeal surpassed its goal. International disaster responded to the tsunami and the Pakistani earthquake. This was in addition to funds that went directly to the synods, congregations, and individuals who were impacted. This is indeed a church of abundance, and we celebrate this outpouring of gifts. Thanks be to God for the generosity of this church!

Feltman is sensitive to the fact that LDR's commitment to long-term recovery doesn't garner the attention of other relief efforts. Consequently, there is the misperception that Lutherans aren't involved in disaster relief. Untrue. Working through existing LDR affiliate agencies, LDR's model of response has four core components:

- Hardship grants of $300 to $500 per family for the first 60 days to supplement other support available from FEMA, Red Cross, or other local agencies.
- Spiritual and emotional care, especially for those serving in caregiver roles. Professionals in mental health and chaplaincy

are contracted to provide spiritual and emotional support through the long recovery process.

- Volunteer management and coordination. The vast majority of the work force to clean up after a disaster and do the rebuilding of buildings and communities is provided by volunteers. These volunteers come for a week to several months to help out. They need to be scheduled, housed, fed, and supported in their work.
- Long-term recovery and case management. After a disaster, people are often dazed and have trouble knowing what they want or need or how to go about getting it. Case managers work as advocates for individuals and families to help them decide what they need to put a new life in place.

Despite extensive disaster experience and expertise, Feltman says that LDR is learning and designing new ways to carry out these four core components. This is largely because LDR affiliate agencies were forced to evacuate along with everyone else, and the unprecedented damage the storms inflicted on facilities, infrastructure, and networks throughout such a large region made it extraordinarily difficult to respond through normal channels. Feltman explains:

It really was like setting up operations in a third world country. The first weeks of this [disaster] were chaotic and ever-changing. As new assessments were completed and information gained, we modified our response to meet the context.

We've learned a lot in the past twenty-four months that has sharpened our skill set immensely. We offer preparedness grants to our LDR affiliates so they may work with congregations and communities to prepare for disaster.

Each of our affiliates employs a disaster coordinator so relationships and communications are well established prior to a disaster occurring.

Because the recovery work is in an area prone to hurricanes, there is concern for the safety of volunteers and staff. Plans are in place to evacuate hundreds of volunteers to safety in a short amount of time.

LDR is absolutely committed to helping restore lives overwhelmed by the disaster. From September 2005 through January 2007, LDR will have disbursed $18 million. From September 2005 through April 2006, LDR staff has documented over 500,000 volunteer hours. ELCA colleges and campus ministry sites brought 1,100 students to the Gulf Coast region to help over spring break 2006.

*   *   *   *   *

Much of the Lutheran Community's response to Katrina and Rita is being delivered through a contract relationship with Lutheran Social Services of the South. (LSSS). Dr. Kurt Senske, president and CEO, notes that the Internet provided individuals with a powerful and expedient means of providing support and organizing relief in the storm's wake. "[The response to this disaster] really has been a million points of light. I think the ability to communicate via the Internet . . . made this possible."

Senske believes that it's important for traditional responders, including LSSS and LDR, as well as the Red Cross, United Way, and even FEMA, to recognize that individuals, working outside of established avenues of response, can make a real difference. "We need to talk about how to incorporate both ways of responding [to disasters] in order to build a more effective model for future responses."

He echoes Heather Feltman's assessment that Katrina created unique challenges, but acknowledges that the storm also provided opportunities to initiate changes to improve future relief and recovery efforts.

> Before Katrina, the funding for disasters only enabled us to have an infrastructure that used part-time staff that had other duties in non-disaster times. Because of the generous funding from many sources in response to this disaster, we now have the funding to provide full-time staff that is only focused on disaster response issues. We are in a much better position to be proactive to respond to future disasters due to this enhanced infrastructure and skill sets.
>
> Katrina really solidified our opportunity to build an organizational structure solely devoted to disaster. . . . In eight months we've gone from two part-time staff to one hundred staff [people] . . . focused on disaster recovery in the Gulf Coast. And we're establishing relationships with Habitat for Humanity, which could increase that effort even more. . . . When all is said and done, the Lutherans will have played an important role in providing help, healing, and hope to those impacted by Katrina and Rita.

Pastor Tom Minor, a retired Air Force chaplain, was appointed to the newly created position of Executive Director for Disaster Relief in the Gulf Coast area in February 2006. He brings to his new role previous experience as a crisis team member assigned to work with families of people killed in the terrorist attack on the Pentagon on September 11, 2001. Pastor Minor notes several challenges for responding effectively to future disasters:

> There is no team of organized responders. The team has to be assembled and developed and that takes time. If it is a large disaster, such as Katrina was, it takes months. We all want a quick fix to the problems, and when that doesn't happen someone has to be blamed. Adding to all of this you need to have the dollars flowing for the long haul, as well. If there is another major disaster somewhere else, that can change where the priorities are and where the volunteers go.

> There are many people today who are surprised when they are told the states affected by Katrina/Rita haven't been totally restored and that the restoration of those states will take ten or more years to complete.

> The communities have to own their own recovery and sometimes that can limit what can be done in a given area. We have to play by the local rules of the city governments. As hard as it is to believe, some of the cities, counties, or parishes have rules that even during the recovery phase will not let you house volunteers in areas that you need to work in. When this happens, you are not only fighting to work the recovery but fighting the city to let you help them recover. It can take awhile to forge all of this into a workable situation.

> I'm pleased to be helping to rebuild the Gulf Coast, getting the pieces in place, helping the children of the victims. It's exciting to see what we're able to do to get everything up and running. We need to thank the volunteers and those

working with the disaster recovery. They put in long hours and are constantly giving of themselves.

We truly are part of a global village. When Katrina hurt us, more than thirty foreign countries came to our aid with prayers and financial aid. International monetary gifts exceeding $66 million became the Katrina Aid Today fund, which was awarded to the United Methodist Committee on Relief (UMCOR). UMCOR then distributed the funds through a grant process to other non-government agencies to use for case management work with the families hurt by Hurricane Katrina.

Lutheran Disaster Response was one of nine agencies chosen to receive a grant from Katrina Aid Today, and was awarded $6.6 million. Heather Gatlin, a former LSSS staff member, was called back to LSSS in January 2006 to coordinate the Katrina Aid Today program for LDR. he reports about two-thirds of LDR's $6.6 million portion is being spent on case management in Texas and Louisiana, with forty percent allocated to Houston, forty percent to Baton Rouge, and twenty percent to New Orleans. The remaining funds have been allocated to seven other states where New Orleans residents are still living in temporary situations. Through these funds, LDR is working directly with approximately 6,800 families.

Gatlin explains that Katrina Aid Today is designed to be volunteer-driven. The goal is for every paid professional case management staff person to be supported by four volunteers whose responsibilities will include, among others, data entry, home visits, and referrals.

Another example of how the church is saying yes to its baptismal calling is through congregational partnerships that provide much-needed financial help and sweat equity for recovery and rebuilding. Grace Lutheran Church in Conroe, Texas, said yes when asked, "Would you be willing to open your doors as a Red Cross Shelter? We desperately need a shelter in your area." For the month of October 2005, Grace provided a "home" for homeless people from New Orleans and other areas hit by two hurricanes less than a month apart. And when the last of the "tenants" moved on and the shelter was closed, the people of Grace asked, "Okay. Now what?"

According to Grace pastor, Mark Rinehart, the thought was, "Let's pick one congregation, support it, its members, and its neighborhood. Then they will be strong enough to serve their neighborhood." Grace Lutheran Church in New Orleans, which was flooded with over seven feet of water, seemed a good choice. Pastor Rinehart and Bill Richardson, "a member of [Grace-Conroe] with a big heart for New Orleans," visited the city in November. "It was simply overwhelming," Pastor Rinehart says. "House after house, block after block, mile after mile of stinking devastation. New Orleans was at the time the largest toxic waste dump in the world. We visited Gethsemane Lutheran Church in Chalmette, another church in New Orleans whose facility was completely devastated. I cried as I walked through their sanctuary. On Sunday we worshiped with the people of Grace, New Orleans, in a funeral home."

During the six-hour drive back to Conroe, the two talked about what should happen next and decided it was important to get other congregations involved. Later in November, Pastor Rinehart wrote a letter to every congregation in the ELCA named "Grace"—all 383 of them—and invited them "to pray, to give, and to come down and help if they were so inclined [sic]." And so Operation Saving Grace began. Over the next weeks and months, people of "Grace" from all across the country contributed more than $100,000 and performed countless acts of kindness to help a sister church get back on its feet.

A few months later, Pastor Rinehart initiated a similar partnership between Gethsemane Lutheran Church in Chalmette and other churches with the same name. Although there are only 32 Gethsemanes, the response was proportionate to the earlier endeavor, raising approximately $10,000 to assist in rebuilding the ELCA congregation that sustained the most extensive damage in the disasters of 2006.

"The power of the Spirit is present in the work of the church. We truly are Christ's hands and feet," contends Pastor Rinehart. "Sometimes, it takes a crisis to shake us out of our isolation and remind us that we are part of a bigger community. It takes a disaster to teach us how to work together in our denominations and in our communities. My prayer is that what we have gained might not be lost, but rather be compounded. How blessed it is when we live together in unity."

*   *   *   *   *

The Holy Spirit has moved individuals, congregations, synods, and agencies and institutions of the church to respond with arms wide open to the needs of an entire region of the country impacted by disaster in triplicate. Among those responding is Thrivent Financial for Lutherans. Marilyn Chassie, manager of Lutheran Community Services in the Mid-South Regional Financial Office, lives in Mandeville,

Louisiana, and is a member of Hosanna Lutheran Church. According to Chassie, the corporate office had just completed a revised plan for Thrivent's national disaster response program when Katrina hit:

> The plan is [that] after the President of the United States declares a national disaster, a team of Thrivent leaders allocates dollars as relief funds designated for a specific disaster. These funds provide an opportunity for individual members to supplement their charitable gift for disaster recovery to LDR or the large Lutheran church body's relief programs. In addition, disaster relief dollars are allocated to supplement fundraising efforts of service teams (community or congregational) that raise funds for the Thrivent region where the disaster occurred. For Hurricane Katrina, Thrivent allocated $2 million to supplement member gifts to church disaster relief programs and Thrivent's regional program. In addition, Thrivent allocated an additional $5 million for Gulf Coast recovery under the Thrivent Builds with Habitat for Humanity partnership. With the gifts of our members, this means that Thrivent allocated over $11 million toward gulf coast recovery from Hurricane Katrina.

Chassie lauds the response of Thrivent members on a local, regional, and national level:

> At first we didn't know this was the worst natural disaster in U. S. history. As we watched with horror at what was happening in New Orleans, people around the country reached out with unprecedented generosity. Within days of Katrina,

church bulletin inserts were distributed and Thrivent's supplemental gift forms were completed by members from Lutheran congregations throughout the country. Within six weeks of the disaster, the major Lutheran church bodies had received sufficient funds from Thrivent members to request 100% of the supplemental allocation. According to LDR figures released recently, over $24 million have been received by LDR to date; we know that at least $6 million was a result of Thrivent member participation.

At the Thrivent regional level, approximately $3 million was received as a result of chapter and congregational efforts. Chassie says that by working through direct providers, the focus has been to use these funds to support infrastructure and efforts at volunteer work sites, providing bunk beds, RV hook-ups, food for volunteers, and shower stalls, as well as purchasing supplies to help with mucking out and rebuilding ravaged homes.

"I'm so proud of what we've done, not just us, but . . . a vast community of volunteers." Chassie says, "I get three or four calls a week from volunteers who want to send money or come back again."

But she also sees some need for improvement. There have been frustrating breakdowns in communication.

We need to network. People have come with skills that our communities and people aren't ready to use. We have received valuable supplies, and we are still working hard at developing storage facilities. There is still so much to do! We need to do a better job of connecting resources with unmet needs.

We're not actually in the disaster ministry as Thrivent Financial for Lutherans. We're in the business of helping those who are directly engaged in disaster work. We're in the business of connecting our volunteers with ways that they can fulfill their desires to make a difference in the lives of others.

Another form of disaster response is the ministry of Camp Noah. Melanie Davis, national director for field operations for Camp Noah, recounts that Camp Noah began as a pilot project in 1996 to help youth process the trauma of tornadoes in Arkansas. Davis was a seminary student when a tornado struck her parent's Arkansas home. She spent the summer assisting with the first Camp Noah, and began working with the ministry permanently the following year. "When the floods hit the Midwest [in 1997], we knew we had to do something to help the children through the various stages of disaster and recovery."

Davis arranged for two women, Stephanie Hardy and Kathryn Anderson, to write and later revise program curriculum, which is based on the story of Noah and the flood but focuses on the hope of restoration and God's abiding presence even in the worst of times.

"Our goal," Davis says, "is to make Camp Noah as portable as possible so that we can help as many children as possible all over the country and even internationally." In 2005 there were thirty-four camps offered in Florida, Alabama, and Puerto Rico. Because there is such a huge need for Camp Noah following Katrina and Rita, initial plans were to provide one hundred camps. But after reviewing the infrastructure needed to support such an effort, the goal was reduced to fifty camps for 2006. They were planned from Houston where many Gulf Coast children still live after evacuating their homes. Some twenty-five teams, trained in other parts of the country, provided staffing for the camps.

Dr. Terry Germann used another Bible story to help traumatized residents and staff evacuated from Bethlehem Children's Home in New Orleans to Bokencamp Home in Corpus Christi, Texas. Katrina and the flooding that followed destroyed the facility of this residential ministry founded in 1881. Germann, a pastoral counselor, used the story of Peter walking on the water to help the children process what happened to them. He asked, "Who came through the water to rescue you when the water was rising?" Because children often respond to pictures better than words, Germann, assisted by his daughter, Amanda, used art therapy to help the children express their feelings, and to provide reassurance. "Our goal," he explains, "was to help the children achieve resiliency."

With his background as a consultant to Lutheran Disaster Response and as part of the crisis management international team following the 9/11 attack in New York City, Germann's concern isn't only for the victims of disaster, but also for the volunteers who play such an instrumental role in disaster recovery. He warns that because disaster recovery work is so intense, volunteers need to monitor themselves and be careful not to over-function. Germann teaches that healthy helping comes from compassion and is the result of seeing the world as a place of abundance, "People believe there's enough," he explains, "[so] I can be generous and share. The river can flow out toward others rather than worrying about what it will be bringing into me. The focus is on what the recipient needs and how we can help them achieve it. We help people identify the need and walk with them to meet it. This builds hope." He cautions, "If we decide their need without asking, we encourage dependency and are telling them we know their need better than they do."

Germann says that unhealthy, over-functioning compassion is based on low self-esteem and the need to be needed in order to feel okay. It stems from a belief that "there's something wrong with me." But when a caregiver overdoes it, it encourages the receivers to under-function, and this weakens their ability to help themselves and know the satisfaction of doing so.

Disaster response professional Kevin Massey agrees that volunteers need to be prepared. "[Models have been prepared] to provide a network of board certified chaplains who are trained to serve in times of disaster and who can train others at the local level to provide emergency and spiritual care. This is organized through the National Volunteer Organizations Active in Disasters (VOAD)—a network of non-governmental nonprofit agencies—many of them being faith-based."

Massey came to Lutheran Disaster Response in December 2005 with a background that includes serving as an emergency room chaplain at a Chicago hospital and helping provide spiritual and emotional care in New York City after 9/11. Like many people drawn to help in a disaster, he's had personal experience. "My family was impacted by a tornado many years ago, so I had seen devastation to a city. But it was just stunning to see the extent of this [disaster]. It just goes on and on and on for miles."

Massey says that some people really can't handle the emotional demands of disaster work. "We have to screen people because in times of disasters there are always a few who are voyeuristic and self-appointed responders who aren't trained and who aren't prepared for the level of trauma they'll encounter. They come on their own and they mean to help, but the boundaries get fuzzy and they can end up doing more harm than helping. They can harm themselves and those they are seeking to help as they become traumatized themselves."

As the recovery work for this disaster continues, and as volunteers come on board to help with future disasters, it is so important to do this with the understanding that we are all called to do our part and trust that God is asking others to do their part too.

The many volunteers who have come at their own expense have given so much to inspire hope. One woman describes seeing "the Lutherans come flowing down the street from that big bus—a sea of humanity." She marvels that these wonderful people totally gutted her house in just two days. Truly Katrina and Rita have drawn out the best that thousands of compassionate people have to give.

Discussion questions

1. What situations in your life have left you feeling compelled to take action? When you have you responded spontaneously to some crisis situation without taking time to think through the details? How did that work out for you? Would you do it again? Why or why not?
2. What is your main source of information about local, regional, or global disaster relief efforts?
3. If you were in charge of responding to a major disaster in your area, what steps would you take?

4. If you or your loved ones were victims of a major disaster, what kind of support do you think you'd want?

Reflection starters

Reflect on one of the following scripture passages, using the suggestions for reflection included in Chapter 1 (see page 28).

Matthew 7:7-12—Ask and you will find.

Matthew 25:35-36—I was hungry and you gave me food.

Mark 4:30-32—Parable of the Mustard Seed

Luke 7:37-38—Give and it will be given to you.

Action items

1. Learn about the emergency resource agencies in your zip code area. If this information isn't already posted at your church and in your home, prepare a flyer with contact information and make it available for future reference.

2. Do a little Internet research on the work of major disaster responders such as Red Cross, United Way, Lutheran World Relief, and Lutheran Disaster Response.

3. Do you know the names and non-emergency phone numbers of your local police and fire department personnel? With a little online research or a few phone calls, you can identify who these first responders are. They'd appreciate a thank-you note from a grateful citizen.

5

Resurrection and New Life:
The Body of Christ Reaches Out and Rebuilds

"But there are also many other things that Jesus did; if every one of them were written down, I suppose that even the world itself could not contain the books that would be written."
—John 21:25

The Chinese symbol for crisis is made up of two like shapes that nestle together to form a circle. One represents danger. The other, opportunity.

Within weeks of the storms, signs of life began sprouting up amidst the debris. Wounds that will last for years—even lifetimes—began to heal. People who lost their past began to look forward.

The Lutheran church in America is stronger now because of new relationships born as congregations—large and small, urban and rural—welcomed newcomers. The church is stronger, too, because of mutual support offered as servant groups continue to trek to the Gulf Coast to help with the massive clean-up effort.

The United States, a melting pot comprised of people with diverse ways of thinking, acting, and organizing, is different, too. We have seen that collectively we have a deep capacity for compassion and hope, but we've also learned that, as strong as we are, we need help from our global neighbors . . . and when we do, they respond.

Eight months after Katrina, Easter came, reminding us once again that love is stronger than hate. Hope is stronger than despair. Life is stronger than death. In churches throughout the ravaged region, believers gathered to worship the Risen Lord.

The people of Grace Lutheran in New Orleans, who had worshiped since the flood in the Lemana-Pallo-Fallo Funeral Home, returned to their building on Easter Sunday. Grace's church council president, Dr. James Wee, published the good news in an e-newsletter dated May 8, 2005:

> So, how is Grace-NOLA doing? The last month has been great! We did in fact hold Easter services at Grace, and they were awe-inspiring. You may remember that the buildings were first deemed safe, having been gutted, cleaned, and the mold declared officially gone. The only electricity in the buildings is the contractor's line, so there is no air conditioning. Since our temperatures have been in the 80s regularly by late morning this month, this is a concern. But, open doors and fans helped immensely. The week after Easter, we held services at Grace a second time and voted unanimously to return for a third and fourth week. In fact, with no dry wall covering the cinder block walls in the sanctuary, the electric organ [donated by St. Paul Lutheran Church in Rosenberg, Texas] sounded fabulous, as if we were in a big, old, European church.

The people of Gethsemane Lutheran Church in Chalmette, Louisiana, where the flooding was particularly severe, gathered in a large tent in the parking lot on Palm Sunday because mold deemed the building unsafe for worship. Gethsemane member Gaby Haze shares her delight at being "home":

> And God saw that it was GOOD.
>
> I can not come up with a better word, and GOOD seems to be the ultimate as God himself used it in the beginning, when creating paradise.
>
> A total of 112 people gathered to worship our Lord with victory palms on the beginning of this Holy Week. We have to order more chairs as we had only 80. I thought 100 bulletins (graciously donated by Pastor Jim Abbott, Brenham, Texas, and typed, copied, and folded by Christ the King in Kenner) were too many. We ran out of coffee, and people just hung around till high noon or later. So glad many of you brought your own chairs; some still stood through the service. God provided the most beautiful weather for this special day.

New partnerships have been forged, including several ecumenical relationships, as congregations and communities look to the future. Dr. Wee reports in the Grace Lutheran newsletter:

> I have been working with Pastor Dan (Duke) to see if Grace-NOLA can provide leadership for the rebound-ing Lakeview faith community. Catholic, Presbyterian, Baptist, Episcopal, and Methodist churches are down Canal Boulevard from us, within a half-mile. We are working to

find a team of parishioners to contact these congregations to see if we can support each other and coordinate our activities, bring a larger presence to the Lakeview faith community. Obviously, if schools, businesses, and churches reopen, there will be increased incentive for people to move back or rebuild in Lakeview.

Congregations that weren't as severely impacted are finding new mission and ministry foci. This is the case for Love Lutheran Church on the West Bank in New Orleans, served by Pastor Scott Landrum. He reports, "After the storm, our congregation began asking, 'What is something we can do that others aren't already doing? We have FEMA and Red Cross and Lutheran Disaster Response and others all doing relief and recovery work. What do we have to offer?' We focus on Word and Sacrament. There's no reason to reinvent to wheel. This is what we do."

Pastor Landrum says that a new opportunity has arisen from the congregation's focus on Word and Sacrament. "The [Texas–Louisiana Gulf Coast] Synod . . . identified us as a base for a new ministry. In July, a Vietnamese pastor, Rev. Thuong Le, [became] pastor of . . . outreach ministry to the Vietnamese community. Many of the Vietnamese have had to relocate. They were established on the East Bank, then had to evacuate, and are now resettling on the West Bank, near where we are located. We have a $50,000 grant to do . . . outreach ministry to this community."

New ministries develop in surprising ways. Pastor Jim Shears, now commuting from Memphis to serve Gethsemane Lutheran in Chalmette, explains, "We've been sort of thrown into ministry with the fishing villages south of us. One of our members started . . . taking down supplies to them. She met someone else and they began partnering on this effort. Then somehow we ended up with a $7,000 grant from some Brittney Spears Fund through someone who knew someone who was connected to the fishing villages."

In St. Bernard Parish, where Gethsemane is located, 76 percent of the houses are abandoned. Even at the rate of 65 houses per day, demolition of the 3,500 destroyed residences is going to take time. Yet the people are rebuilding. Pastor Shears reports, "We have about two-thirds of our congregation back somewhere in the region. Others are as far away as Oregon or North Carolina. . . . St. Bernard Parish just appointed a new Chief Administrative officer, Dawn Santalucito—who happens to be a member of [Gethsemane]. God is directing us. Our plan is to rebuild our church as fast as we can so we can have a ministry by people who've been through the storm for people who've been through the storm. I'm excited. We're rebuilding to be able to house volunteers. God has really blessed us."

Bishop Ronald Warren of the ELCA Southeastern Synod recognizes the need for continued ecumenical efforts to assure that focus stays on the Gulf Coast after the media pulls away. To that end, judicatory heads in Mississippi gathered together at the end of 2005 to address concerns that the old paradigms for disaster relief and recovery were not working. While referring to Lutheran Disaster Response as "a bright shining star" in their commitment to stay the course throughout recovery, there is concern that the federally mandated Red Cross model for disaster relief isn't good enough in disasters of the magnitude of Katrina.

Pastor Dan Duke of Grace Lutheran Church in New Orleans echoes the notion that the Gulf Coast will need help from outside for a long time to come. Pre-Katrina, Grace had a membership of about 400 with average worship attendance of 160. The congregation is averaging about sixty-five percent of that now, and its budget is about a third of what it was. Pastor Duke reports, "We're getting a lot of support from a lot of places. The Synod is paying my full salary right now. We're getting gifts from all over the country—a $50,000 gift from a church in Florida; $7,000 from a congregation in Pennsylvania—the money continues to pour in. I went to preach at a congregation in North Carolina and they presented me with a check for $10,000. I know we can rebuild, but I don't know if we can sustain the church after that. We cannot budget the gifts; we assume they are one-time gifts."

A significant number of congregations in the Midwest who weathered severe flooding in 1997 are sending Grace monthly support. Having been through a major disaster themselves, they understand well the long road ahead. Pastor Duke continues, "I think it will be at least ten years—I've heard estimates of up to twenty-five years—to recover from this." In spite of it all, he says he's hopeful.

*   *   *   *   *

Though the public is most aware of the impact of the storm and ensuing floods on the New Orleans area, Katrina inflicted incredible damage to communities along the Mississippi coastline. Judy Bultman, a member of Bethel Lutheran Church in Biloxi, reports that people with nowhere else to go continued to live in homes washed off their foundations by the storm surge, or on porches that survived even though houses were destroyed, or in tents pitched where homes used to stand.

"A friend of mine told me that she felt lucky and guilty at the same time because their bedroom is still standing," says Bultman. "She, her husband, and her daughter have been living in that one room since the storm. But, she has a sister whose house was directly across the street and was demolished. Her sister has been pleading for her and her family to stay in that one room. There are probably thousands of families like this living in 'what is left' simply because there is nowhere to rent, buy, or move . . . especially for the poor. Not only do they not have a home, their automobiles have been destroyed and they have no way to get anywhere to get relief."

Bethel Lutheran Church, served by Bultman's husband, Pastor Gerald Bultman, didn't sustain extensive damage, so the needs of the larger community became their focus. "We [took] our ministry . . . into the streets where the people are living. Slowly people began coming . . . shoeless adults and children shivering in the cold, reaching up, begging for our quilts and meager food supplies. We emptied the truck in a matter of moments and then began to take orders for much needed items like shoes, jackets, more quilts, and always detergent, detergent, detergent!"

The relief phase is gradually moving into recovery, Bultman reports, but the need remains great. To help get out that word, she worked with others to create a DVD presentation showing what the region is up against, and she takes that message with her as she speaks to groups throughout the southeast.

The need also remains great for congregations and communities impacted by Hurricane Rita in September 2005. Bernard Scrogin retired in July 2005 from the staff of Lutheran Social Services of the South (LSSS) and moved with his wife, Betty, to Fredricksburg, Texas. They were visiting their daughter in

Connecticut when Katrina started coming in. He remembers thinking, "I knew LSSS would need help, so I wasn't surprised when Mark Minnick (the LSSS staff person charged with responding to disasters in the Gulf Coast region) called and asked me to come back to help. I talked it over with Betty and she said, 'If you're going, I'm going.' I . . . started in September with no discussion about how long the work might last.

"It's been frustrating, but the Long Term Recovery Committee for the area is now formed, so we finally have some consistent leadership. Southeast Texas Interfaith Organization (SETIO) is a brand-new nonprofit formed just to coordinate the response to the damage caused by Rita. There is a paid staff person in place and we're beginning to clarify who is going to be doing what. In April, Trinity Lutheran in Orange created an office for me at the church. Someone helped us find a rental house. We're finally starting to get organized and better coordinated."

Looking to the future, Bernard talks about a vision for the area. He says it's crucial that the local community own the recovery process. "It's been hard to pull people together. But some of the racial and economic barriers are breaking down and people are starting to work together. This is an opportunity for the different faith communities to sit down together and have a vision for the future. Not everyone will join in this effort, but at least people are talking to one another."

*   *   *   *   *

Eight months after the beginning of events that changed the landscape and lifestyles of millions of people, Easter came to the Gulf Coast. I met with the Louisiana pastoral leaders sixteen days after the Festival of the Resurrection. After some initial fellowship time, we moved into the worship space of Christ the King in Kenner, Louisiana, whose facility had not suffered significant damage. We sang a hymn, read scripture, and prayed. Then Ron Unger, pastor of Christ the King and dean of the Louisiana Ministerium, invited us to preach the sermon together by taking turns sharing a summary of the Easter sermons we had preached two weeks earlier in our respective worship settings. Those who were retired or serve in specialized ministry were asked to recall the sermon they had heard in worship on Easter Sunday.

It was fascinating to hear how each person chose a particular aspect of the Easter proclamation to emphasize and reflect upon. It was fascinating to realize how full the scripture stories are in terms of what can be foundational in telling the old, old story in many different ways.

Most pastors whose congregations had been impacted by Katrina talked about how living through the storm and floods made the Good Friday to Easter story come alive. The "shared sermon" was a word of grace, hope, and renewal given as gift to each other. The use of the Katrina experience to make a clear connection to the heart of the Christian message provided the real presence of the rescuing, resurrecting God among us.

Indeed, God was in the raging waters, just as God is, now, in the debris of demolished homes and bruised lives. God continues, over and over, on a daily basis, to interrupt and intercede in the context of brokenness and destructiveness. When death has tried its hardest to cut us off from our creator and redeemer, God in Christ blew open the tomb and let the winds of eternity blow through.

Those who lost everything and had to be evacuated from their homes and communities found themselves welcomed and embraced by rescuers who reflected a resurrected people themselves. There are enough storms in life to bring each of us to a moment when we need to be rescued. Whatever form rescue takes, in the actions of God's people, Jesus' words can still be heard above the storm. "Peace, be still." It's that hope that offers us a new beginning and carries us into a future held securely in God's hands forever.

"What then are we to say about these things? If God is for us, who is against us? . . . Who will separate us from the love of Christ? Will hardship, or distress, or persecution, or famine, or nakedness, or peril, or sword? . . . No, in all these things we are more than conquerors through him who loved us. For I am convinced that neither death, nor life, nor angels, nor rulers, nor things present, nor things to come, nor powers, nor height, nor depth, nor anything else in all creation, will be able to separate us from the love of God in Christ Jesus our Lord" (Romans 8:31, 35, 37-39).

Discussion questions

1. What hopes do you have for yourself for the future?
2. When and how have you seen good follow disaster?
3. Have you experienced something that seemed to be a complete failure that turned out to have a happy ending?
4. What events or experiences in the midst of loss have helped you be aware of God Immanuel—God with you?
5. What gives you energy to try new things and move in new directions?

Reflection starters

Reflect on one of the following passages, using the suggestions
   for reflection included in chapter 1 (see page 28).
Psalm 30—Weeping may last for a night, but joy comes in the
   morning.
Genesis 9:12-17—God's sign of the covenant.
Isaiah 65:17-18—Behold, I will create new heavens and new
   earth.
Matthew 6:25-34—Therefore, I tell you, do not worry about your
   life.
Revelation 21:1-5—Behold, I make all things new.

Action item

Change is an inevitable part of life. Sometimes the change
is forced from without by storms and circumstances beyond
our control. Sometimes the changes are gradual and predict-
able, such as the different physical, social, mental, and spiritual
changes we experience as we age. Sometimes the changes are
intentional—planned and wanted shifts in one or more aspects
of our lives. Take a survey of your current circumstances to
determine whether there are changes you wish to make in any
area of your life.

Look at the chart on page 90. For each aspect of your current life, rate how satisfied you are, using a scale of 1–5:
1 very dissatisfied
2 dissatisfied
3 okay
4 satisfied
5 very satisfied

Note any steps you want to take to maintain or improve that aspect of your life.

Dimension of Life (Wellness)	Level of Satisfaction	Plans for the future
Physical		
Mental		
Social/Family		
Spiritual/Emotional		
Vocational/Work		

Additional Resources

Web Sites

www.elca-ses.org. This Web site for the ELCA's Southeastern Synod gives updates on progress in Mississippi and other sites impacted by Katrina, along with links to other disaster response sites.

www.elca.org/disaster. The official ELCA Web site's disaster page provides an update on the church's recovery efforts for Katrina and Rita, along with other disaster recovery work around the world.

www.futurewithhope.org. This special website established by Rob Moore, assistant to the bishop of the Gulf Coast Synod provides updates about the status of the congregations and people of the Gulf Coast, ways to volunteer and to donate, and links to other related resources.

www.ldr.org. Learn how Lutheran Disaster Response is structured to respond to disaster, find resources for disaster preparedness, prayers, volunteer opportunities, and other disaster related information.

www.lsu.edu. The Web site for Louisiana State University in Baton Rouge has many resources that offer research on the cause and effect of major storms, the effect on the people impacted by them, photos of the damage and clean-up operations, and other data about the storms.

Books and Videos

Bade, John McCullough. *Faith in the Midst of the Storm.* DVD. A pastor in Baton Rouge, he has had a significant role in both recording the tragedies of the storms and assisting in the recovery process from them. A thorough overview of the damage inflicted by the storms and the recovery process through photo images and hymns of hope. Available through www.mc-bade.net.

Brinkley, Douglas G. *The Great Deluge: Hurricane Katrina, New Orleans, and the Mississippi Gulf Coast.* New York: HarperCollins Publishers, 2006
Tulane University historian writes about the events of the hurricane and flood from the perspective of political decisions before and during the crisis.

Harbaugh, Gary. *Act of God, Active God: Recovering from Natural Disasters.* Minneapolis: Augsburg Fortress, 2001.
A resource to help individuals and groups grapple with what to think about God during times of natural disasters. Available at www.augsburgfortress.org.

Massey, Kevin. *Light Our Way*
A resource guide by Kevin Massey, assistant director for ELCA Domestic Disaster Response, commissioned by the National Voluntary Organizations Active in Disaster for those who provide spiritual care in disaster. Available through the Lutheran Disaster Response Web site, www.ldr.org.

Meeting God in the Ruins: Devotions for Disaster Relief Volunteers. Chicago: ELCA Division for Congregational Ministries, 2003.
Written by ELCA Domestic Disaster Response team members to support disaster relief volunteers and help them process what they

see and the stories they hear as they move into a disaster area to assist with recovery. This resource helps them prepare to help others. Available at www.augsburgfortress.org.

New Every Day: Forty Devotions for Disaster Survivors. Chicago: Lutheran Disaster Response, 2005.
Written for disaster survivors, the guide is a collection of 40 devotions, Bible verses, prayers, and Lutheran Disaster Response contact information. Available at www.augsburgfortress.org.

Rogness, Peter, and Nancy Maeker. *Ending Poverty: A 20/20 Vision.* Minneapolis: Augsburg Fortress, 2006.
Two staff from the St. Paul Area Synod describe the systemic circumstances of our culture that perpetuates situations like the desperation seen among the poor in the flooding of New Orleans. The book lays out a plan that emphasizes how we are all part of one community. Available at www.augsburgfortress.org.

Rose, Chris. *1 Dead in Attic.* New Orleans: Chris Rose Books, 2006.
A series of Post-Katrina stories by New Orleans Times-Picayune columnist Chris Rose, with photographs by British photojournalist Charlie Varley. A poignant, tragic, and sometimes even humorous collection of essays from August 29, 2005, through New Year's Day, 2006. Available at www.chrisrosebooks.com.

VanDuivendyk, Tim P. *The Unwanted Gift of Grief: A Ministry Approach.* Binghampton, N.Y.: Haworth Press, Inc., 2006.
Written by a Houston chaplain, this book helps those lost in the wilderness of loss and grief as well as the professionals who care about and for them. Available at www.HaworthPress.com.